RICHA in Longford, Tasmania, in 1961. His six novels are published in forty-two countries and have received numerous honours, including the 2014 Man Booker Prize for *The Narrow Road to the Deep North*. He is the Boisbouvier Chair of Australian Literature at Melbourne University.

BEN QUILTY was born in Sydney, Australia, in 1973. The recipient of numerous art prizes including the Doug Moran National Portrait Prize, Archibald Prize and the Prudential Eye Award for Contemporary Art in Singapore, his work is represented in major national and international collections.

NOTES ON AN EXODUS

AN ESSAY BY RICHARD FLANAGAN

ILLUSTRATIONS BY BEN QUILTY

VINTAGE BOOKS
Australia

A Vintage book
Published by Penguin Random House Australia Pty Ltd
Level 3, 100 Pacific Highway, North Sydney NSW 2060
www.penguin.com.au

Penguin
Random House
Australia

This essay was originally published in *The Guardian*.
With special thanks to Charlotte Northedge, Emily Wilson, and
Nikki Marshall.

First published by Vintage in 2016

Addresses for the Penguin Random House group of companies can be
found at global.penguinrandomhouse.com/offices.

National Library of Australia
Cataloguing-in-Publication entry

Flanagan, Richard, 1961– author
Notes on an exodus/Richard Flanagan; Ben Quilty (illustrator)

ISBN 978 0 14378 235 3 (paperback)

Refugees – Syria – Anecdotes
Refugees – Lebanon – Anecdotes
Refugees – Greece – Anecdotes
Refugees – Serbia – Anecdotes
Syria – History – Civil War, 2011– – Refugees – Personal narratives

Other Creators/Contributors: Quilty, Ben, 1973– illustrator

362.87095691

Cover illustration of Heba © Ben Quilty
Cover design by Christa Moffitt, Christabella Designs
Typeset in Bembo by Midland Typesetters
Printed in Australia by Griffin Press, an accredited ISO AS/NZS
14001:2004 Environmental Management System printer

Penguin Random House Australia uses papers that are natural, renewable
and recyclable products and made from wood grown in sustainable
forests. The logging and manufacturing processes are expected to
conform to the environmental regulations of the country of origin.

For Conny Lenneberg

In January 2016 Richard Flanagan and Ben Quilty travelled to Lebanon, Greece, and Serbia to follow the river that is the great exodus of Syrian refugees.

1

'Yesterday was the funeral,' Ramadan says. 'It was very cold. We make sure Yasmin always has family around her.'

Yasmin wears a red scarf, maroon jumper and blue jeans. She is small and slight. Her face seems unable to assemble itself into any form of meaning. Nothing shapes it. Her eyes are terrible to behold. Blank and pitiless. Yet, in the bare backstreet apartment in Mytilene on the Greek island of Lesbos in which we meet on a sub-zero winter's night, she is the centre of the room, physically, emotionally, spiritually. The large extended family gathered around Yasmin—a dozen or more brothers, sisters, cousins, nephews, nieces, her mother and her father, Ramadan, an aged carpenter— seem to spin around her.

And in this strange vortex nothing holds.

Yasmin's family has come from Bassouta, an ancient Kurdish town near Aleppo, and joined the great exodus of our age, that of five million Syrians fleeing their country to anywhere they can find sanctuary. Old Testament in its stories, epic in scale, inconceivable until you witness it, that great river of refugees spills into neighbouring countries such as Lebanon, Jordan and Turkey, and the overflow—to date more than a million people—washes into Europe across the fatal waters of the Aegean Sea.

'We were three hours in a black rubber

boat,' Ramadan says. 'There were fifty people. We were all on top of each other.'

The family show me. They entwine limbs and contort torsos in strange and terrible poses. Yasmin's nine-months-pregnant sister, Hanna, says that people were lying on top of her.

I am told how Yasmin was on her knees holding her four-year-old son, Ramo, above her. The air temperature just above freezing, the boat was soon half sunk, and Yasmin wet through. But if she didn't continue holding Ramo up he might have been crushed to death or drowned beneath the compressed mass of desperate people.

Then something happened.

Ramadan looks up. He seems seventy but is fifty-four.

'We lost track of where the children were,' Ramadan says.

2

'What was Syria like?' I ask Ibrahim.

We sit in a transit centre in north Serbia through which thousands pass every day, the twelve-year-old Ibrahim drawing a picture of home.

'Black.'

Like the other children drawing their memories of Syria, he reaches only for black and blue pencils, the darkest colours.

'Because of Daesh everything is black,' Ibrahim explains.

His picture is a mini-*Guernica* of body parts. He finds a red pencil and draws blood.

'Do you think that there will be light now?' I ask.

'It was smoky, black, because of the bombing,' Ibrahim says.

I ask him what other colours were in Deir ez-Zor.

'There were no other colours.'

He's preoccupied with his drawing, and he says to the table, to the drawing, to the paper: 'In Europe I see every colour.'

'Name one colour for Europe,' I say.

Ibrahim looks up. He wears a blue fleece cap with earflaps pulled hard down over his face that accentuates a gaze too intense, too piercing for someone so young. He has the look of a medieval child beggar. There is a scab on his upper lip; his chipped and scattered teeth roam the room while he talks.

'White,' Ibrahim says.

3

'My favourite colours,' Raghda says as we sit down in her tent in a Lebanese camp, 'are the fire colours.'

An elegant, poised woman in her mid-twenties, Raghda wears a pink-and-scarlet dress and hijab ornamented with embroidery and divided by a black scarf.

'Why fire colours?' I ask.

'Because,' Raghda replies, 'they're about rebirth.'

A sewing machine sits in one corner, an unexpected interruption to the normal austere emptiness of refugee tents. Raghda teaches sewing and, for $10 a piece, makes dresses for others in the camp. She points to a wall where several hang, waiting to be picked up. Her clothes are vibrant, resplendent with colour, bling, beads and embroidery.

Raghda speaks gently, softly smiling, as she tells of how she has a degree in 'women's art'—fashion design, sewing, drawing—and hoped for a career in fashion. Then, Daesh arrived—as incomprehensible to

Raghda as it is to so many Syrian refugees, as inexplicable as a tsunami or an earthquake—and turned her home town of Raqqa into its capital.

'Daesh came suddenly upon us,' Raghda says. 'We don't know from where they came. They wore scarves around their faces, they only knew a few words of Arabic—they were Chechen, Chinese, Afghans, Americans, Somali, Pakistani—they wore masks.'

Her husband, Mohamed, saw Daesh kill a man in front of him.

'Mohamed didn't look,' Raghda says. 'But the blood follows him.'

We are a few kilometres from the Syrian border, high up in Lebanon's Bekaa valley. In mid-winter the Bekaa is a bleak world of muddy, littered flatlands bounded by vast snowy ranges. The dreary soot of snow clouds briefly parts for a hard red sun that rolls like a severed head over Syria.

The ploughed winter earth is fallow save for one crop that sprouts like weeds: the plastic-clad hovels that run in colourful ribbons everywhere.

The plastic takes various forms: white polytarp, bags, the bright buntings of discarded billboards promoting perfumes and smartphones, honed images of corporate beauty: Kate Moss, Christian Dior and the iPhone 6s. Only when you come close are you able to see this bitter harvest for what it is: endless shantytowns—'camp' seems too orderly a word for their broken disorder—in which survive perhaps half a million Syrian refugees.

Perhaps more.

Depending on the wealth they bring with them or their lack of it, another million Syrian refugees can be found living in culverts, ruins, slums and better-quality apartments throughout Lebanon—a nation itself of only 4.5 million. No one knows the exact number anymore as the authorities stopped registering refugees a year ago and closed the borders a few months later.

But still they come.

Forced to choose between life and death, they choose life, even when it means living for years in shelters that are half-hovel, half-tent, framed of scrounged timbers and clad in a motley of plastics. In these shanties pride does daily battle with poverty and the elements.

A weak electric bulb will throw a dull light over the plank-raftered ceilings above that leak when it rains and drip condensation when it doesn't. Below long shadows will crawl over unwaterproofed slabs that wick dampness from the wet earth all day, every day. Sometimes there is a small cathode-ray television, and always a charger for the ubiquitous smartphone that even the starving possess. Neatly arrayed on the ground are fetid floor mats and a few mattresses and cushions on which all sit. In the centre a small iron box burns either oil or the scraps of wood that can be scrounged—chipboards, melamines, treated pines—the damp, slightly warmed air riddled with the razored scents of pungent carcinogens and heavy metals.

The alternative is hypothermia.

'After a time there was no work,' Raghda continues, 'there was no money in Raqqa, no fuel for cooking. We couldn't even afford to buy potatoes.'

Because Raghda worked with naked mannequins, a crime punishable by death, there was always the danger she would be killed by Daesh.

'I was very afraid,' Raghda says. 'Daesh

make any excuse to kill you. You must dress as they say—even the men. If you swear they cut you in half. Whoever treats humans like they do is not human.'

The aerial bombings by the Russians and the Assad regime grew worse. Mohamed saw the school next door bombed; their balcony was blown off by the force of the explosion and shrapnel pierced doors inside their home.

'Ever since,' Raghda says, 'Mohamed has had nightmares in which the planes come to kill us all.'

Caught between the cruelty of Daesh and the savagery of the Assad regime, and with Raghda heavily pregnant, the couple finally fled.

Like so many others, they are heavily in debt, owing $1500. They pay $550 a year for renting the tent; $20 a month for electricity that powers a light and a phone charger; and they must also find $50 every month for the excess electricity to run the sewing machine.

'Still,' Raghda says, 'here in Lebanon I feel free. In Syria I was forced to wear a black burqa all the time. Here I can go back to our tradition.'

I am not sure what tradition means.

'Colour?' I ask.

'Yes,' Raghda says. 'Colour.'

The blizzard blows. The tent moves. She looks up.

'In the night,' Raghda says, 'we are frightened. My family is still in Raqqa. My happy dreams are of going home—always us going home.'

Two weeks ago—three weeks after they escaped to Lebanon—their baby daughter was born, one of 40,000 refugee babies born every year in Lebanon, stateless, paperless, vaccine-less, with little chance of a formal education. Raghda breastfeeds her in front of us.

'She is called Sulaf,' Raghda says. 'It means sunrise.'

4

A blizzard was coming to the Bekaa and the mountain passes leading to the coast and Beirut would soon be blocked by snow. It felt like a prison world, another world, a lost world, an inverted Shangri-La where only misery reigned; hundreds of thousands of hovels housing half a million lost souls no longer allowed a home, a country, a life. Perhaps it was all these things and more. Twenty minutes' drive away was a wilderness of war called Syria. The Bekaa felt a borderland in every sense—between Syria and Lebanon, between affluence and abject poverty, between oppression and freedom, between despair and hope, between life and death.

And like every borderland the frontier was invisible and the line was ever-moving. Sometimes the line wound its way down refugee camp laneways of filthy mud, ankle deep, past children playing in icy puddles in bare feet, past the empty faces of the lost and the drowning, and into the ramshackle tents of the wretched of the earth.

And in one of these there lay in its most distant corner, on a mattress on the damp floor, a young man, Mohanad, pale, hairless, staring into some mid-distance. His face is the colour of something old and congealing. Mohanad is twenty-four and he is dying of diabetes and kidney disease. Two weeks earlier Mohanad tried to hang himself so that he would no longer be a burden to his family.

Zahir, an articulate twenty-seven-year-old woman and Mohanad's sister-in-law, sits opposite with Samir, Mohanad's mother. She explains how Samir has had open-heart surgery and needs medications. They cost $400 a month, Mohanad's $200. Other than her husband Jostin's occasional earnings, the family make do on aid money of $5 a week a person. They go short of food to buy medicines for Samir and Mohanad and to keep the primitive iron heater in the middle of their tent burning night and day so that mother and son can stay warm. Zahir stretches her arm out to indicate a very small, quiet child in the shadows; her own six-year-old son, Eid.

'Because he doesn't eat,' Zahir says, 'Eid isn't growing.'

But even with such sacrifices there still isn't enough money and so they borrow. The family now owes $1000. Every day the men to whom they owe the money come and ask for it. And every day, from the damp floor on which he lies, Mohanad yells, 'Take me! Take me!'

They laugh about this, and then Zahir talks of how Syrian government MiGs bombed their home and bombed the hospital so that Mohanad could no longer get dialysis in Syria.

'We couldn't go on,' Zahir says. The family fled Raqqa in 2012.

'We had a lovely life,' Mohanad says, his voice strangely strong, as though he wants to be heard far beyond his miserable tent.

'We never expected to be here for four years,' Zahir continues. 'It's in God's hands what happens.'

'My health was good,' Mohanad says.

Today Mohanad's health is not good. He returned an hour ago from having dialysis in a Lebanese hospital and he is very tired. He has to have dialysis three times a week, for which an NGO pays $100 a session. But after this year the NGO will no longer pay for his dialysis.

I don't ask what they will do then. What can they do? There is no money. There is only debt, and the debt they have is unpayable.

'He's brave,' Zahir says.

'Yes,' I say.

'I suffer a lot because there's nothing I can do,' Zahir says. 'He can't see. You hold his hand so he knows that you're there.'

'If I can say anything it is this,' Mohanad says. 'We need help. We need medications.'

Nobody speaks. I want to be able to promise such things, or something, or anything, but I fear any promise will be broken, or too late. And I sense Mohanad knows all this.

'I dream of returning to Syria,' Mohanad says. 'I see everything when I close my eyes.'

The rain thrashes at the tent. The polytarp cracks and slaps. A repressed reek of stale ammonia grows.

'Do you see the sun in your dreams, Mohanad?' I ask.

'Yes,' Mohanad says.

The chill is growing all round and rising from the floor. Something is biting my thigh. There is no escaping the claustro-phobic despair of the tent.

'I miss my homeland,' Mohanad says.

'Life is very hard,' Samir says.

'I miss the olive tree I used to sit under,' Mohanad says. 'I miss my father's graveyard.'

'The heart,' Zahir says, 'the kidney. Very hard.'

Mohanad has a strong, insistent voice. But now he says nothing. He stares into the distance.

I am searching for another question. There are no questions. There are no answers. Please God, I think, give me words. There are no words. I can see no further than Mohanad. I want to keep talking so we can pretend—what? That there is hope? That writing this later will mean something? I look around.

Suddenly Samir, who has been quiet until now, speaks up.

'I feel my heart is burning,' she says. 'For my son's situation. For my situation.'

Samir starts to sob. Zahir is crying.

Elias the videographer stops filming. He starts building a boat out of paper for little Eid.

'Let's sail it to Germany,' Samir says.

The tent leaks, the storm builds, we leave them to their fate, relieved, ashamed to be once more in that dreadful rutted mud outside.

5

Fiad is a truck driver from Deir ez-Zor. Thin-faced, moustached, he wears the chequered keffiyeh on his head, a traditional Arab. Fiad is constantly smiling.

'Before the revolution we lived well,' he says, offering me tea in his Bekaa valley tent. 'But Deir ez-Zor was rich and important to Daesh. Daesh told me I had to fight for them or they'd kill me. So I fled, paying $500 to the people smugglers.'

And Fiad smiles again, offers me a cigarette, lights one for himself, and goes on.

'I had eight children. Daesh killed seven. My heart is not working anymore. I don't care about myself anymore. I don't care about Daesh anymore. I have one child left in Syria. Life here is so hard because we left our country, our loved ones. There is nothing more precious than your country, your home.'

Fiad is staring into his tent's iron fire box.

'If you lose your country,' Fiad asks the fire, smiling, 'tell me, where can you find it?'

6

'When I lie down at night I swear it's a dream or a nightmare and I will wake up back home,' Feisal says. 'When I dream I dream of my lands, my apple and peach trees. We are picking the peaches.'

I compliment him on his tent, its neatness, its hospitable welcome, the tea we are drinking. He smiles wryly, and in reply points a smouldering Gauloise up into an exclamation mark, a gesture of futility. He tells me of his home, a village near Homs that his family established five generations ago. He was the headman.

'It was a beautiful village,' Feisal says. 'I used to provide for all my family, my brothers and their families as well.'

He had cows, 100 hectares of fruit trees, three children at school. They would pick 200 tonnes of peaches every year.

Feisal says he would love to show me his lands. Instead he must stay up all night scraping snow off the roof so that it doesn't collapse.

A small man with a sagging face disguised by a moustache and the arabesques of cigarette smoke he weaves by waving his smoking hand, Feisal is dressed in a formally western style, wearing grey pants and shirt and black leather jacket. He has met me in the manner of the mayor he effectively is of another shantytown we are visiting.

'The day I left my village the sky was on fire,' Feisal says, 'the earth was on fire. I left my cows, I left my sheep, I left my fruit trees.'

The fumes of formaldehyde, phenol and cyanide drift in waves from the ubiquitous cast-iron heater to mingle with the smoke of his Gauloise and the damp funk of the cheap rugs in his tent to make an acrid fug, at once dull and sharp, as Feisal tells of how fifty villagers walked for three nights, hiding by day. They ran out of bread but had water. Arriving in the Bekaa, they camped on a friend's property, where, unusually, they pay nothing in rent. Over time, his whole village joined him, and today they number 250.

Feisal has saved his village, now transplanted, and watched it grow. But there is no pleasure or happiness in it, only despair and fear. Thirty children have been born since they arrived. He says it is very hard when children are born because of the extra costs. His youngest son, Mouyad, is eighteen months old. Feisal worries that he'll become homeless, an itinerant illegal labourer earning $2 a day.

He cannot afford to register Mouyad or any of his family as refugees with the Lebanese government—a cost of $2000 for his immediate family—and so, Feisal, as an illegal refugee, rarely ventures away from the camp.

'We sit here all day,' Feisal says. 'We can't go out unless it's a funeral or we'll be picked up by the Lebanese army. We go crazy.'

He's grateful to Lebanon for hosting them. But, he says, a life without working is nothing.

'There's always hope,' Feisal says. 'If there wasn't hope we'd be dead. But this is not a life here. At war you have only yourself to worry about. But here you have many people to worry about. Every day this is the war. Here, every day.'

Feisal takes us for a tour of his camp. He wants to show us how they live. Down a muddy lane he takes us into a tent which inside, astonishingly, is revealed to be a school. A score of small children sit at low bench tables, listening attentively to their teacher, a young woman called Naja. The schoolroom is a triumph of magical thinking: there are children's pictures on the wall, some charts, a small bookcase with books. It is one of the most moving rooms in the world.

They learn English, mathematics, Arabic, geography and history, with thirty older children attending in the morning and thirty younger ones in the afternoon. I ask Naja what they thought on the day they left their village.

'We didn't think,' Naja says. 'We were terrified. We fled. Shells and missiles were hitting our village. We daydream about missiles. We cry. My heart starts burning when I think of this.'

One small boy jumps over a table, pulls his jumper and shirt up, and turns his back to us to show us where shrapnel wounded him when he was three. His classmates shriek with laughter.

The children talk of their dreams. Winsam dreams of Syria. Hani wants to be a doctor. Daline wants to be a doctor. Kinana wants to teach Arabic. When I ask them why they would choose these jobs they all answer to help rebuild Syria.

'We only teach them to keep hope alive,' says Naja.

Feisal, until this point impassive and silent, standing back, mutters something.

I ask the translator what he said.

'This is not a school.'

'It's a beautiful school,' I say. 'I don't think I've ever seen a more beautiful school.'

Feisal shakes his head, and for the first time I sense something other than pride and patience, the indomitable will of the survivor, the public stoicism of the headman. He seems angry, enraged in a quiet way. He points a Gauloise stub to the plastic lining flapping in and out in the winter winds and shakes his head.

He holds his smoking hand to the ceiling that might cave in tonight or tomorrow, to a world that might continue and shouldn't, that may or may not be here in a few hours, to a waking dream that is a living nightmare, and it is clear how much he hates it all, how he longs simply to wake up and once more see his peach trees in fruit. He mutters again, and the translator translates again.

'Can't you see, this is not a school, Feisal is saying,' the translator says, a little embarrassed. 'Look, he is saying, where is there a school? It's a joke.'

7

Zara's black scarf wraps around her mournful face. She is sixty years old and demands I see inside her tent. It's eight in the morning, a blizzard has come and gone, not as snow as feared, but as sleet and rain and wind. Every tent has leaked. Inside Zara's is a dirty puddle, ankle deep, covering the entire floor. Her bedding sits on its side, wet, and, who knows in such weather, in a damp, leaking hovel, how long it will take to dry? Zara suffers from arthritis in her knees and has a chest infection. She has lived here for four years. She stares at me, her face a question to which I can make no answer.

'Of what do you dream?' I ask.

Zara starts coughing, a deep wet bark, and for a long time is unable to stop.

'Of returning home to Syria,' Zara says finally, when she has caught her breath. 'Of peace and of happiness.'

8

Six-year-old Omar coughs again, and tells us he also collects plastic bags. One large garbage bag of compressed plastic bags is worth 80 cents, he says, enough to buy a pack of four flatbreads.

'Omar had lambs, sheep and chickens to play with at our home,' his father, Hamidi, says. 'Any sort of food.'

Hamidi, an illiterate farm labourer in his

mid-fifties, has a long face like a noble piece of beef jerky and the seeming tolerance of a man who can wait several lifetimes. His family's story unfolds in such a matter-of-fact and easy way that it is almost possible to miss the hopelessness of their world. It's early morning in the Bekaa and we are sitting in a freezing shanty clad in hessian potato sacks. In it live the ten-strong family of Hamidi and his wife, Kartana, who have fled the horrors of Aleppo.

As we talk, Omar sits on the floor drawing machine guns and grenades. Other than the pencils and paper we have brought, and his own glass jar with half a dozen marbles, Omar has no toys. He dreams of going back to the farm his father laboured on near Aleppo. He has bad dreams of people coming into their homes with guns. Most mornings Omar walks two kilometres to the vegetable store in the nearby town, collects food scraps off the floor, walks home, and the family boil up the scraps for lunch.

'If you came to visit us in Syria we would have killed a lamb for you,' Kartana says. 'Our life before the war was amazing.'

'We didn't know how to close a door,' Hamidi says. 'We were blessed, our land was blessed.'

'We were safe,' Kartana says. 'We had nine children. The best thing is safety, that when you sleep you sleep safely.'

'We opposed the regime in our head,' Hamidi says. 'Ours was an opposition of the mind, not of weapons.'

But eventually the weapons of others found them and they too had to flee. Hamidi was kidnapped, ransomed, given up as worthless, and only reunited with his family two years later.

The $5 aid for each person a week they now receive only runs to a maximum of five people a family. They are a family of ten seeking to live on $100 a month—or $10 each a month—and whatever else they can scrounge.

'I have to feed ten people every day,' Katana says. 'We live on bread, tea and bread.'

'We all work in summer in the fields,' Hamidi says, 'but now in the winter there is no work.'

'If there is not enough food,' Kartana says, 'Hamidi and I don't eat.'

'What will you have for lunch?' I ask.

'We don't know,' Kartana says.

The family's only other source of money during winter is what their nine-year-old son, Jamal, makes as a welder. Jamal works seven days a week, leaving at 8 am and returning at 6 pm, for which he earns $3 a day. His employer keeps back half his pay each week to make sure he returns to work.

'If you don't have patience,' Hamidi says, 'you don't have religion. The most important thing is our dignity. If we have that we can survive on bread and water.'

But dignity is dissolving in the mud and sleet of the Bekaa valley, where kids run around barefoot, families starve to buy medicine and nine-year-olds work seven days a week in welding shops.

I am told how Nazir, their thirteen-year-old daughter in a pretty green dress, is about to be married off to her fourteen-year-old cousin. There is no one else of their tribe in their refugee camp and Kartana feels their daughter isn't safe if left alone. And they can't feed her. Now someone else, she says, can provide for her and protect her. It's the best they can do for her, for themselves. Nazir's prospective husband works as a shepherd, sleeping with his flock. Their wedding will be a small celebration in the tent of potato sacks for an hour with perhaps fifteen people.

'We will make her hair look pretty,' Kartana says.

'In Syria it would be seven days of singing, dancing, eating,' Hamidi says, holding his hands aloft as though an alternative wedding might still be found and caught falling from the sky above. 'All the tribe would come,' he says. 'Six hundred people!'

When I ask Nazir how she feels about her impending marriage, she smiles and looks down at the baby she is holding. Her gaze wanders to the damp floor mat. The baby coughs and coughs, and Nazir says nothing.

'Sometimes a month passes and no one enters our tent,' Hamidi says. 'But in Syria there are always people. My mother is still alive but sick in Syria. I would like to see her again. Thank God for everything.'

Hamidi rarely leaves the tent of potato sacks. He doesn't like it outside. He has sat inside for two years. Waiting to return to his home in Syria.

Omar coughs deep and hard. The baby coughs. Kartana says Omar has bad dreams of being covered by an avalanche, a mountain of snow coming down from the ranges that wrap around them, burying them all forever. In his dream only he survives, without family.

'When you see the mountain ranges around you like prison walls what do you feel?' I ask Hamidi.

'I pray.'

'What do you pray, Hamidi?'

'May God help the righteous and keep us safe,' Hamidi says. 'People are being slaughtered in Syria and no one knows why.'

The baby coughs and coughs.

'We're lost now and we don't know our destiny,' Hamidi says. 'But we thank God for our freedom.'

The baby won't stop coughing.

9

In a Serbian transit centre near the Croatian border, six-year-old Heba is drawing. A purple parka hood and knitted red beanie frame a small, olive-skinned face. Her face seems to swim with smiles. Neither shy nor assertive, but simply herself, Heba is one of those children about whom people say there is something special. Nothing in her face or demeanour gives the slightest indication that she is haunted in her dreams of planes coming to bomb her and her family.

I ask her about her home in Deir ez-Zor.

'I love it,' Heba says.

But her family home was blown up by a Russian bomb.

I tell her she can draw a new home now.

'I only want a non-Daesh home,' Heba says.

Ahmed and Alfaf, Heba's parents, have lost everything. Ahmed wears a black beanie, a blue scarf, a black parka. At thirty he is a man in his prime. A police officer with a strong face and a powerful body, something in him nevertheless seems broken.

'Daesh have been in Deir ez-Zor nearly two years,' Ahmed says. 'They started cutting heads off. Schools were closed and only religion taught, and even that only until they are ten. Then the children are recruited as child soldiers.'

Alfaf says she could no longer work as a teacher as all the schools were closed.

They heard the plane engines continually, as Assad regime and Russian planes took to bombing the town twenty-four hours a day. Then their home was blown up.

'There was a smell of smoke like a fog, the smell of earth,' Ahmed says. 'My first feeling was that our home was ruined, then I realised that our children had no future, no education. I knew we had to leave.'

They fled Deir ez-Zor carrying their children, abandoning on the road the few bags and possessions they had taken with them. Fearful of being returned to Syria by the Turkish authorities, they resolved to attempt to make it to Europe. Frightened of the possibility of drowning, Ahmed paid a people smuggler $2100 to get himself, Alfaf and their three children to Greece, the condition of his payment being that there would be no more than thirty-five people on the boat. They were allowed to take one five-kilogram backpack.

'What did you take?' I ask, wondering what a life looks like when it is reduced to five kilograms.

'A change of clothing for each of the three children,' Alfaf says. 'Nothing for ourselves.'

When they arrived for their departure it was to discover there were sixty people on the boat. Ahmed gets out a Samsung Galaxy and shows me a short video of their crossing. The grossly overloaded boat wallows in a heavy sea, its inflatable black rubber pontoons sitting a mere handspan above the waterline.

Another refugee had told me how on the boat they saw death in each other's eyes. It's not a figure of speech. An old man wraps his arm as tightly around an inner tube as a frightened toddler does around a mother's leg. Waves break over terrified faces grimly set against a future that may prove as fatal for them as it has for so many.

'We were very afraid,' Alfaf says. 'We held our children above us so they would not be crushed.'

Alfaf has extraordinary eyes—large, dark, open—that seem amplified by her hijab. They glisten with tears as she speaks of the boat. Her only thought as they made the perilous crossing was for her children.

On 15 January, five days after they walked out of Deir ez-Zor by night, they landed in Lesbos. They were wet through and the Red Cross helped them, giving them clean, dry clothes. They were hungry and the Red Cross fed them.

'I knew my children were safe,' Alfaf says. She finally smiles. 'We were happy to be in a normal country. We heard a plane and the children were afraid. "Don't be afraid of the planes," I told our children. "There's

Yasmin

Edris

Ibrahim

Six-year-old Heba's picture of a barrel bombing by a helicopter gunship.

no Daesh here, no killing here. They won't drop bombs. We're safe. It's normal."

'If we could,' Alfaf says, 'if peace came, we would return home.'

'Syria is the best,' Ahmed agrees.

Heba is drawing a picture in black watercolour pencil of her dreams. Like all the other children's pictures it is only black, except for the blood. It shows one of the Assad regime's helicopter gunships dropping barrel bombs. On the ground are dead, bleeding bodies.

'Has she seen these things?' I ask Ahmed.

'They all have,' Ahmed says.

'What happens after the bombs fall?' I ask Heba.

She answers without looking up from her drawing.

'Children die,' the small child says, smiling.

10

'Ramo was a cheerful, happy boy,' Ramadan says. 'Like Edris.'

No echo of that Edris—of the happy, cheerful man—can be found in the grieving, broken man opposite me. Edris is a labourer. A thin young man, he has haunted eyes, as if they're covered in kohl. Dead eyes. He sits on a chair, leaning so far to one side it is as though at any moment he might lose balance, fall, and not know how to get back up.

Sitting next to him in the chill Mytilene apartment, his wife, Yasmin, holds her space with an extraordinary and terrible dignity that is almost regal. She says nothing and simply stares ahead. Her eyes are something you wish to look at and something which everyone avoids making contact with. The best you can do is steal glances. The tragedy has made her something else. The destiny that has brought her far from her home to Lesbos, and this backstreet apartment and the room in which we all now crowd on a bitterly cold January night, is meaningless to her.

Like Edris, who looks as though he might at any moment tumble to the floor, like Mohanad with his unseeing eyes seeing all, perhaps she doesn't see the room in which we sit, the family crowding everywhere, the pregnant sister sitting next to her, and us, strangers from another universe. I wonder if Yasmin and Edris are here at all, if they have ever been here at all in this strange new dream, but rather remain on a sinking boat in a chill sea, alone, searching the world for Ramo and then seeing him and trying not to believe. Edris's face is blue. Are they still there with Ramo?

'What did Ramo look like when you found him?' I want to ask, I need to know. But I say nothing, of course, how could I? Ramo, I know, looked like Edris's eyes.

'Life was good, beautiful,' Ramadan is saying. 'We all lived together in a big Arabic house.'

Yasmin liked her room, her furniture for the wedding, wooden furniture made by Ramadan, the olive-green sheets in which she slept.

She had been married to Edris for two years before the birth of their son, one year into the war. They named him Ramadan after her father, and in the family he became known as Ramo.

As Ramo grew, the war went on and life became ever harder and more dangerous. They were becoming hungry; they were confined to their house, there was no milk for the children. Most of the time

Edris couldn't reach work because of the fighting. Scared of snipers and explosions, he forced himself to leave the house to get nappies and food for Ramo.

'Lots of people died,' Ramadan says. 'Sickness, lack of medication. We didn't want to face the same fate. It reached a point where we couldn't feed our children. It was a collective decision. After many days of debating we decided it was better to die drowning than by shelling and starvation. We sold what we had and borrowed money. I would not leave my family behind, not one.'

Twenty-three of his family fled together. They experienced many things but their talk returns to only one.

Their boat was sinking in rough seas when a rescue boat from Lesbos turned up. It came close and its bow hit them mid-boat, rupturing a pontoon. The freezing seawater rushed in and the flooded, grossly over-crowded boat began to sink. People fell into the sea.

It's possible to imagine the panic.

Or impossible.

Mohamed, a well-built adult son, tries to describe what the experience was like.

'I know how to swim,' he says, 'but it was so cold'—he suddenly throws his arms across his chest in a spasming clutch—'I couldn't. And the lifejackets the smugglers sold us,' he adds, 'were useless.'

Lesbos's fatal rocks are an orange rind of thousands upon thousands of lifejackets abandoned by refugees, so many that an orange ribbon between the sea and the island is visible from the air as you fly in. That afternoon, standing by the Aegean Sea, I had ripped one such lifejacket apart. Inside was open-cell foam of a type used for soft packaging.

It was so soft I could tear it. I put a piece in the sea and felt it swell, absorbing almost as much water as a sponge. I squeezed it and watched the water drip out. The people smugglers sell these fakes to refugees for $50 a piece—death-jackets, each an elaborate, murderous deceit.

And so too, I suppose, was the one Ramo wore.

No one says anything. Not them, not me. There is a strange, frightening silence. And in that room, at that moment, I found myself part of something that was at once a transcendent grace and a terrible despair. I knew I now needed to ask about the exact details. That was my job. Where was Ramo at this point? Who was holding Ramo? I knew these details would matter to people who read this, that this is what I have travelled across the world to hear, and it is this which I must write.

But I cannot speak.

And every question I formulated seemed an unfair accusation, a grotesque judgment. I wanted to say only one thing. A small, human thing. That I was sorry.

But it was Ramadan who finally spoke.

'Only when we were all finally on the rescue boat did we see him,' Ramadan says.

Ramadan, alone, bravely keeps on. I wonder if he—father, grandfather, patri-arch—who, grieving perhaps as much as Yasmin—for her, his daughter; for Ramo, his grandson—if he must for their sake not allow himself the trappings of grief.

'We lost a child,' Ramadan says. 'But we survived.'

Ramadan didn't sound callous. He sounded like one man trying to hold the many together, to assuage the terrible guilt they all seemed to share, to find some piece of wreckage to which they might cling and not all drown with Ramo. By it he didn't mean something terrible and selfish but rather, I felt, that the family, the clan—the basis and centre of their lives, their only compass, no doubt riven with rivalry, resentments and feuds, and perhaps even hate, but also bound by necessity, obligation, kindness and love—that this had survived, and that this must go on.

I don't ask what happened next.

How did they pull the small body in? Who held the still-warm wet corpse in their arms in the dark and the cold as the rescue boat turned for Europe? What was said and all that can never be said? I am handed two photos of Ramo. Turning and tumbling in the room's strange maelstrom of grief, I can't see anybody in the photos. The room is a dizzying fall.

And still Yasmin sits there, frozen as Lot's wife.

Kalil, a brother, says how his son Jalun nearly drowned. He too feels guilty, and perhaps hopes for some sort of understanding or forgiveness, but there can of course be none.

'The lifejackets were useless,' says Kalil.

'Yes,' I say. 'Yes, yes.'

'Every day we sit here,' says Ramadan. 'We talk about it and we all feel guilty.'

Yasmin is weeping.

'She's waiting for a painkiller,' someone says.

'I have pains in all my joints,' Yasmin says.

'The doctor is bringing painkillers tomorrow,' someone says.

Hana misses her room, misses her mattress, I read here in my notes. I am not sure who Hana is now. Perhaps another of the small children. I remember faces, so many faces and eyes. Every night now I dream of the camps, the haunted faces of that great exodus. They won't leave me.

'I used to love the sea,' says Kalil. 'Now I hate it.'

'People think they know what is coming,' Mohamed says.

'In Bassouta we had a house full of friends and family,' Ramadan says. 'My eldest daughter drowned when she was fourteen. She drowned in a river.'

'I have nightmares,' Yasmin says abruptly. She talks in a rush now, as though we will understand, as though she might. 'I always imagine my little one,' she says. 'I feel I am suffocating. I can't breathe. I feel pain all over my body. Every bone hurts.'

'The doctor is coming,' someone says.

11

At a train station on the Serbian border with Croatia I watched as hundreds of refugees in a long line slowly shuffled towards their destiny. It felt like history and I suppose it was history and is history, and you realise why anyone who has experienced history hates it so. It was minus sixteen, the sky was blue, and there was an odd silence in which all that could be heard was the tramp-tramp-tramp of hundreds of feet somehow falling in time together. It was the sound of history, the most desolate sound I have ever heard.

12

I have a photo in my writing room of my three daughters looking out over a mountain range in Slovenia that leads to the Austrian border—the same mountain pass to which Heba, Yasmin and Edris and Ramadan and so many countless others were now all headed. My daughters' grandparents fled over those mountains as refugees in 1958. And that same year, in a refugee camp in southern Austria, Majda, my wife, their mother, was conceived.

Refugees are not like you and me. They are you and me. That terrible river of the wretched and the damned flowing through Europe is my family.

And there is no time in the future in which they might be helped. The only time we have is now.

25 February 2016

Richard Flanagan and Ben Quilty have donated their royalties from this book to World Vision. You can help Syrian refugees by donating to a charity such as World Vision, and by calling on the Australian government to do more. If the Australian government spent one dollar on helping Syrians for every dollar it has spent bombing Syria, it would increase the amount of aid 800%—from an average of $45 million a year over the five years of the Syrian war, to $400 million—the sum we spent in 2015 waging war in Syria.

Also by Richard Flanagan

FOREWORD BY GEORDIE WILLIAMSON

'BEAUTIFUL AND LYRICAL'
THE WASHINGTON POST

RICHARD
DEATH OF A RIVER GUIDE
FLANAGAN

VINTAGE

RICHARD
THE SOUND OF ONE HAND CLAPPING
FLANAGAN

VINTAGE

'A MASTERPIECE'
THE TIMES

'A WORK OF SIGNIFICANT GENIUS'
THE CHICAGO TRIBUNE

RICHARD
GOULD'S BOOK OF FISH
FLANAGAN

VINTAGE

'STUNNING'
THE NEW YORK TIMES

'COMPELLING AND DISTURBING'
THE ECONOMIST

RICHARD
THE UNKNOWN TERRORIST
FLANAGAN

VINTAGE

RICHARD
WANTING
FLANAGAN

VINTAGE

NEW AND
COLLECTED ESSAYS

RICHARD
AND WHAT DO YOU DO, MR GABLE?
FLANAGAN

VINTAGE

'MAGNIFICENT'
THE NEW YORK TIMES

'DEVASTATINGLY BEAUTIFUL'
THE TIMES

RICHARD
THE NARROW ROAD TO THE DEEP NORTH
FLANAGAN

WINNER
THE MAN BOOKER PRIZE 2014

VINTAGE